unknown
beaver
pond

young beaver's journey

WHAT GOES ON INSIDE A
Beaver Pond?

Becky Cushing Gop • Illustrated by Carrie Shryock

Storey Publishing

IT'S EARLY APRIL, and snowmelt flows down from the mountain ridge into Pleasant Valley Wildlife Sanctuary, rushing into Yokun Brook and the ponds.

Yokun Brook winds for nearly a mile along the base of the ridge.

As the water flows north, it pools in beaver ponds and side channels. The water level rises.

Small patches of ice and snow are still tucked along the water's edge.

During the spring, Pleasant Valley comes alive with sounds and activity.

HONK! HONK! HONK!

Birds return from their winter homes down south. Black bears emerge from their dens.

At the pond's muddy bottom, fish called bullheads stir out of their cold-weather sleepiness. Some dragonfly larvae emerge from eggs underwater. Other dragonflies return north in a spring migration.

A green frog begins looking for a mate.

Salamanders emerge from beneath logs and layers of leaves.

Beavers have stayed active all winter within their lodge and beneath the ice-covered ponds. Now that the pond ice is mostly gone, beaver families get to work on springtime tasks, like repairing their dam.

CHEERILY, CHEER UP,
CHEER UP,
CHEERILY, CHEER UP!

IN THE MIDDLE OF A POND along the Yokun Brook waterway sits a large dome-shaped beaver lodge. It's the biggest lodge at Pleasant Valley Wildlife Sanctuary. A beaver family has used this lodge for the past three winters.

The **LODGE** is built of branches and packed with mud to keep out the rain and snow.

The **AIR VENT** provides fresh air for the beavers to breathe.

The **MAIN PLATFORM** is where the beavers rest and the mother will give birth.

The **SECOND PLATFORM** is where the beavers eat and groom themselves.

The **FLOOR** of the lodge is made of rocks, branches, and mud.

Inside the dark, dry lodge, a young beaver and her family are warm and safe. They share one large sleeping area.

The father and mother beaver moved here from a nearby pond to be closer to a fresh supply of trees—their favorite food.

The young beaver and her brother have spent the past two years learning to harvest food and repair dams alongside their parents. Their little brother and sister have another year of learning before venturing out on their own.

The young beaver is ready to explore.

The beavers' winter food storage, or CACHE (pronounced "cash"), may weigh as much as a large horse.

AFTER FOUR WINTERY MONTHS inside the lodge with her parents and three brothers and sisters, the young beaver wants to stretch her legs and see what's going on outside.

She takes a breath and dives into the water, leaving the lodge through one of the underwater exits. She swims out into the cold pond.

She uses her webbed feet to swim forward and her wide, flat tail to steer. Her tail feels light. The fat stored in it for the winter is mostly gone.

Her oily fur repels the water, so she glides through easily.

She can hold her breath for a long time.

She swims deep, back and forth.

As she nears the edge of the pond, she pokes her head up to listen and sniff. The sounds and smells tell her that winter is ending, and spring is here!

CONK-la-REEE!!

A BEAVER FROM HEAD TO TOE

Beavers spend a lot of time in the water. Their bodies are made for this lifestyle.

HER NOSE AND EARS close to keep out the water.

TRANSLUCENT INNER EYELIDS protect her eyes underwater but let light in.

HER TEETH never stop growing. She has to gnaw on trees to keep them from getting too long.

HER LIPS can close behind her teeth. That keeps her from swallowing water when she carries branches in her mouth.

HER TAIL helps her steer in the water.

OIL from special glands under her tail keep her fur waterproof.

HER SHORT, DENSE FUR keeps her warm.

HER FRONT FEET are like hands, useful for grasping things.

HER WEBBED REAR FEET are designed for swimming. They have a special split toenail she uses to comb and oil her fur.

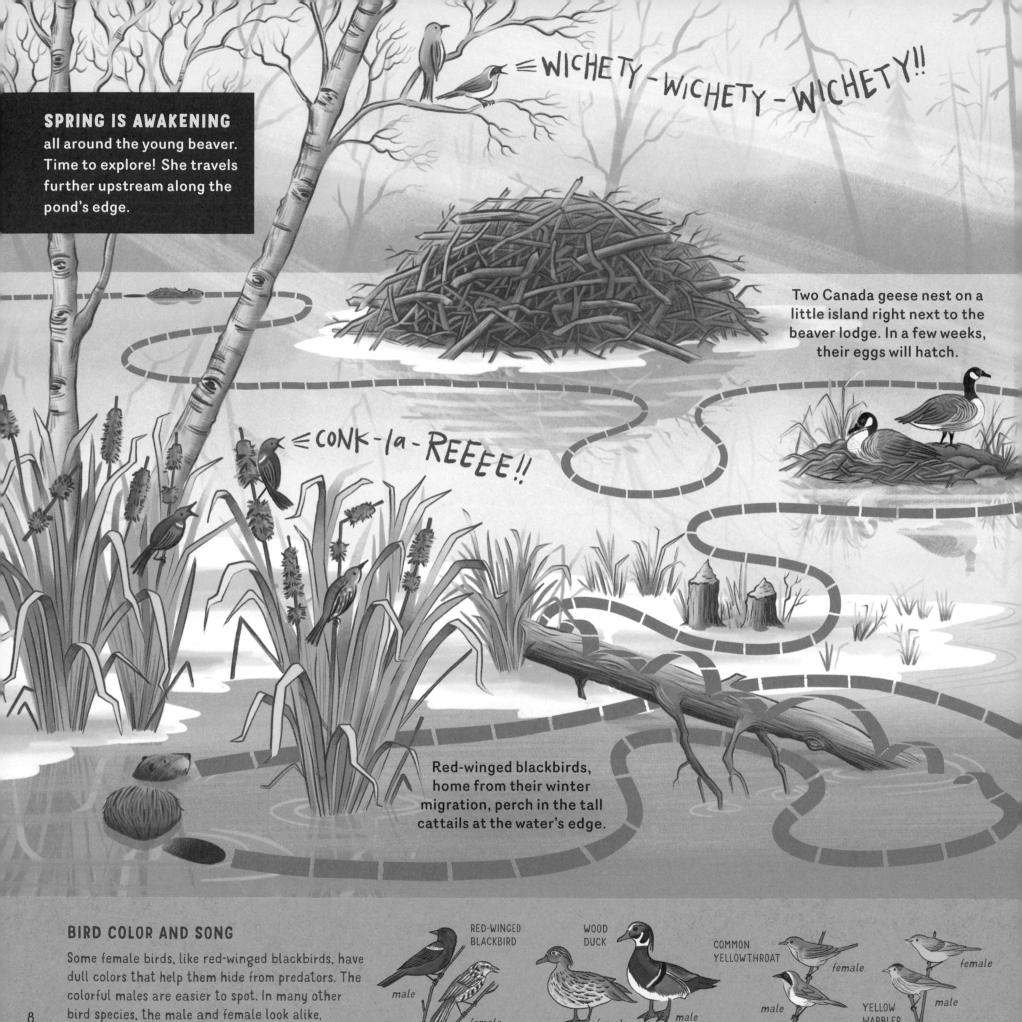

SPRING IS AWAKENING all around the young beaver. Time to explore! She travels further upstream along the pond's edge.

≪WICHETY-WICHETY-WICHETY!!

Two Canada geese nest on a little island right next to the beaver lodge. In a few weeks, their eggs will hatch.

≪CONK-la-REEEE!!

Red-winged blackbirds, home from their winter migration, perch in the tall cattails at the water's edge.

BIRD COLOR AND SONG

Some female birds, like red-winged blackbirds, have dull colors that help them hide from predators. The colorful males are easier to spot. In many other bird species, the male and female look alike.

RED-WINGED BLACKBIRD

male

female

WOOD DUCK

female

male

COMMON YELLOWTHROAT

male

female

YELLOW WARBLER

male

female

8

SWEET! SWEET! SWEET! LITTLE MORE SWEET!

A wood duck nests in a dead pine tree in one corner of the wetland.

Black-capped chickadees are beginning to look for mates and places to build their nests.

CHICKA-DEE-DEE-DEE!!

HEY SWEETIE!

Female and male black-capped chickadees call *chickadee-dee-dee* all year round. In the spring, they switch to another song, one that sounds like *hey sweetie!* Many birds have special songs they sing only in spring, when they are looking for mates or defending territories. Other bird sounds say "danger!"

BLACK-CAPPED CHICKADEE

BELTED KINGFISHER

CANADA GOOSE

GREAT BLUE HERON

THE YOUNG BEAVER EXPLORES the muddy shoreline. The pond and stream channels are lined with hundreds of pointy, chewed stumps where beavers have cut and eaten tree saplings for many years.

Some of the chewed trees have resprouted tiny twigs and will keep growing.

The beaver's favorite trees are birch, willow, and aspen. She doesn't much like the taste of the white pine, although she might eat it when the other trees are scarce.

The mud along the edge of the pond is covered in animal signs left the night before.

As the sun rises higher in the sky, the young beaver returns to her family's lodge. She'll spend the rest of the day inside, resting and grooming.

She climbs onto the grooming platform, shaking off some water. She must keep her fur combed and oiled to stay dry and warm.

Standing on her hind legs, she rubs her face and ears, then cleans her sides and belly with her front feet.

She reaches for the oil glands under her tail and spreads oil across her body, using the split toenail on her back foot like a comb.

Later, she and her siblings will help each other groom hard-to-reach places, but now it's time to nap.

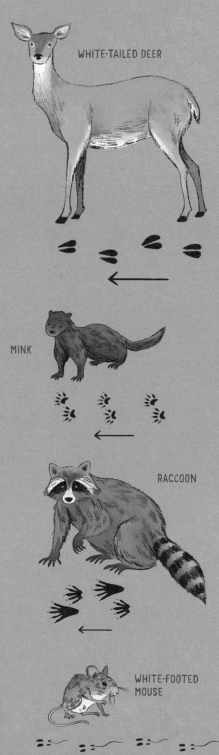

WETLAND MAMMALS

Many kinds of animals depend on wetlands to survive. They often leave signs that they have recently visited.

WHITE-TAILED DEER

MINK

RACCOON

WHITE-FOOTED MOUSE

11

JUST BEFORE SUNSET, the young beaver sits along the edge of the pond eating the twigs of a speckled alder.

Crayfish dart in the shallows a few feet away. Suddenly a blue jay lets out a *squawk!*

SQUAWK!!

At first the beaver does not see any sign of danger. She stops crunching on her twig and sits very still.

She hears a soft rustle of dead grass underfoot, and then she sees it: a small red fox delicately making its way through the grass.

Quickly, she dives into the water, where she'll be safe.

SLAP!

With a loud *SLAP* of her tail she sends a warning to the intruder. Now her family also knows to stay alert.

HUNGRY NEIGHBORS

Beavers avoid large predators, like coyotes and foxes, black bears and bobcats. When danger is near, beavers slap the water with their tails to warn their neighbors.

BLACK BEAR

rear   front

BOBCAT

COYOTE

RED FOX

THROUGHOUT THE SPRING, the beaver family works together to monitor and repair their network of dams. There is always work to do.

old beaver territory

hiking trail

dam

dam

upstream

scent mounds

beaver family lodge

food cache

dam

dam

hiking trail

downstream

vernal pool

14

Every night they check the dams and make repairs. The dams can be damaged in many ways. Rainstorms can make the water rise and overflow the dam.

Sometimes, after a big storm, water breaks right through.

The young beaver and her family also deepen side channels and make pathways to new areas of tasty shrubs.

Upstream, where the beavers used to live, their old dams are falling apart. The beavers let them be.

The water is shallow here, and the trees are growing back. Maybe in a few more years the beavers will return, once there is enough to eat again.

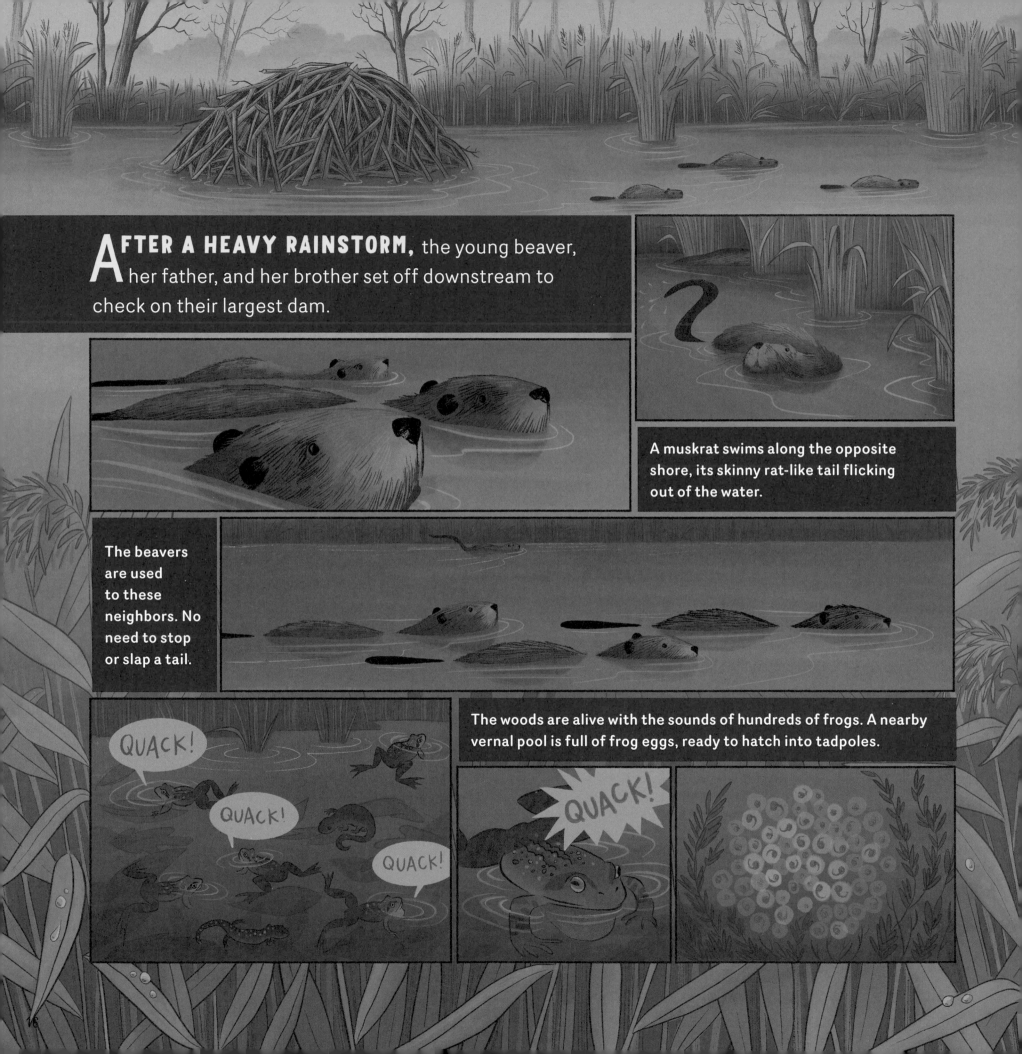

AFTER A HEAVY RAINSTORM, the young beaver, her father, and her brother set off downstream to check on their largest dam.

A muskrat swims along the opposite shore, its skinny rat-like tail flicking out of the water.

The beavers are used to these neighbors. No need to stop or slap a tail.

QUACK!

QUACK!

QUACK!

QUACK!

The woods are alive with the sounds of hundreds of frogs. A nearby vernal pool is full of frog eggs, ready to hatch into tadpoles.

Finally they reach the dam. The beavers listen, smell, and feel to figure out if it needs repair.

The young beaver hears water gushing over the top of the dam. She knows it is the sound of a leak.

GURGLE!

GLUG!

GUSH!

She swims down to the mud at the pond bottom. She scoops up mud with her front feet and carries it back to the dam.

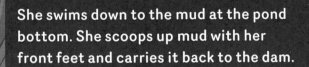

Carefully, she packs the mud into the spaces between branches at the top of the dam. Her brother works beside her. Together, they make the structure stronger and taller.

LIFE IN A VERNAL POOL

On the first warm rainy night in late March or early April, amphibians are on the move. They travel from their winter homes in the forest to lay eggs in nearby temporary ponds, called **vernal pools**.

SPOTTED SALAMANDER

JEFFERSON SALAMANDER

WOOD FROG

SPRING PEEPER

ONE STARRY NIGHT IN MAY, the beaver family returns from repairing a dam to find a surprise. The mother has given birth to two beaver kits!

MEW! MEW!

The kits drink their mother's milk for a few weeks. They can swim at birth but for their first few days, they stay safe and protected inside the lodge.

Then the babies start to venture out of the lodge with their mother. They swim in the water by the lodge entrance.

As the babies grow, the beavers must gather and store even more food. The parents keep the babies close while they work.

MEW! MEW!

The lodge begins to feel crowded. At two years old, the young beaver is ready to leave and start her own family.

JUST BEFORE SUNRISE, the young beaver sets out on a journey. She will travel down Yokun Brook in search of a new home.

PLEASED, PLEASED, PLEASED to MEET-CHA!

She is looking for a place that is peaceful and has plenty of food. She needs either a pond deep enough for a lodge, or a stream she can dam to make the water higher.

She stays in the water as much as possible in case the fox is not finished hunting for the night.

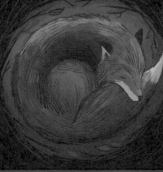

BUZZZZZZZzzz!

She passes a large snapping turtle hunting for food. Snapping turtles eat plants and any small animals they can catch. The beaver is too big to be prey.

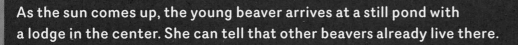
As the sun comes up, the young beaver arrives at a still pond with a lodge in the center. She can tell that other beavers already live there.

These beavers have made dozens of scent mounds around the area. It's like a fence telling her to keep out.

The young beaver can smell that this family has lived here a long time. She doesn't want to fight for this territory, so she moves farther downstream.

SNAPPERS

Snapping turtles have existed since before dinosaurs. They are the largest freshwater turtles in North America.

A snapper will eat anything it can catch with its SHARP BEAK. They are shy but will attack a person if threatened.

It often rests on the bottom of the pond, stretching its LONG NECK to the surface to breathe.

The FEET have SHARP CLAWS for digging.

The LONG TAIL is covered in spikes and used for swimming.

The SHELL and PLASTRON, or under shell, are small compared to its body. Unlike other turtles, a snapper cannot protect itself by pulling itself into its shell.

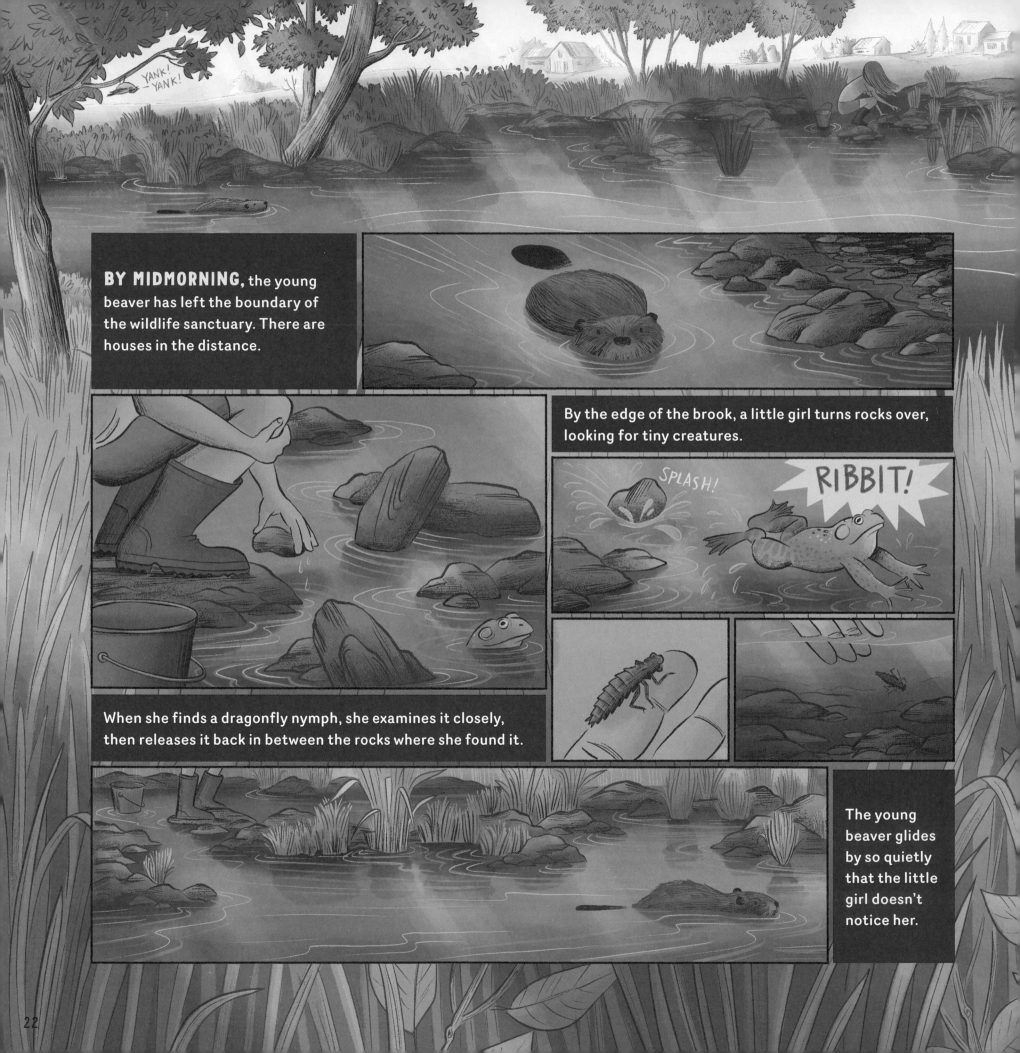

YANK!
YANK!

BY MIDMORNING, the young beaver has left the boundary of the wildlife sanctuary. There are houses in the distance.

By the edge of the brook, a little girl turns rocks over, looking for tiny creatures.

SPLASH!

RIBBIT!

When she finds a dragonfly nymph, she examines it closely, then releases it back in between the rocks where she found it.

The young beaver glides by so quietly that the little girl doesn't notice her.

She is looking for a place farther away from humans, so she keeps moving.

BUZZZZZz!

Downstream, she finds a quiet place in a patch of cattails to spend the afternoon, munching on plant roots in the shallows.

Zzzzzzz...

She will rest now and continue her journey when the sun goes down.

MACROINVERTEBRATES
Small Critters without Backbones

These insects hatch from eggs laid in the water. As adults, they may live on the surface or grow wings and fly away.

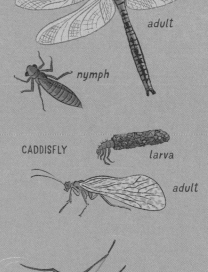

DRAGONFLY

adult

nymph

CADDISFLY

larva

adult

WATER STRIDER

MOSQUITO

STONEFLY

adult

nymph

WHIRLIGIG BEETLE

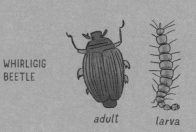

adult

larva

HONK!

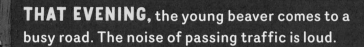

THAT EVENING, the young beaver comes to a busy road. The noise of passing traffic is loud.

SPLISH–
SPLASH!

The stream flows through a metal pipe beneath the road. She would like to stay near the water, but the pipe is dark and she can't tell if it's wide enough to crawl through. It doesn't feel safe.

The young beaver waits until the stretch of road is quiet and then scuttles across the pavement.

The next stretch of the brook is quite different from the home she left behind.

24

The water passes behind a shopping center and alongside a parking lot.

Trash has gathered along the shoreline, and an old shopping cart has toppled down the bank.

The young beaver does not stop to look for food or to explore. This place does not have the habitat that she needs.

CULVERTS FOR WILDLIFE

A culvert is a pipe that transports water underneath a road. Some culverts can also help animals cross safely beneath busy highways.

A **good culvert** is deep enough for fish to swim through and large enough for bigger animals, like bobcats, to pass through. It has a rocky ledge along the side for wildlife to walk on.

A **bad culvert** is small, and one end hangs in midair, so fish and turtles cannot pass through.

IT'S GETTING DARK. Beyond the highway, the brook continues to widen and deepen, and tall trees grow along the banks. The sounds change. Honking cars and squealing brakes fade away. The new sounds remind the young beaver of home.

The beautiful flute-like song of the hermit thrush echoes in the still night.

A northern gray tree frog trills, calling from a secret spot against a tree trunk.

"Who cooks for you?" a barred owl asks.

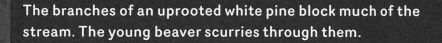

The branches of an uprooted white pine block much of the stream. The young beaver scurries through them.

Somewhere downstream, red fox kits are rolling around and playing by the entrance of their den.

YELP!

YIP! YIP!

A little brown bat zigzags overhead, using **echolocation** to catch insects.

The young beaver stays alert to danger through the cool, still night. As she travels, she wonders: Could this be a good place for a new home?

WHO'S AWAKE?

Nocturnal animals are active at night and sleep during the day. **Crepuscular** animals are most active at dusk and dawn.

These animals have extra-sharp senses to help them hunt and communicate in the dark.

OWLS have extra-large eyes to see well in the dark.

BATS make high-pitched sounds that bounce off flying insects. This **echolocation** helps them capture prey.

MOTHS use their antennae to smell other moths.

Some FISH have feelers for sensing movement in the water.

THE YOUNG BEAVER HAS TRAVELED **ALL NIGHT.** This place feels safe. Before finding a place where she can rest and eat, she explores the pond.

ECK-ECK-ECK!

A belted kingfisher gives a loud rattling call as it flies across the stream.

JUG-A-RUM! JUG-A-RUM!

Bullfrogs call out from their hiding places in the sedges and along the rocks.

RIBBIT!

A clump of water lilies offers shelter and food. In the evening, she'll venture out again.

FROGS, TURTLES, AND SNAKES

Many reptiles and amphibians rely on wetlands for some part of their life cycle. Some lay eggs in the water. Others find food and shelter near or in the water.

BULLFROG

GREEN FROG

PICKEREL FROG

AMERICAN TOAD

The young beaver finds an old dam farther downstream, where the land juts out and forms a little sheltered pool.

GURGLE!

She does not smell any scent mounds, so the other beavers must have abandoned this dam long ago.

Five painted turtles sit perfectly still on a fallen tree, resting in the early morning sunlight.

Water striders and whirligig beetles skid across the surface of the water.

QUACK! QUACK!

Amphibians take in oxygen through their wet, slippery skin. Reptiles have tough, scaly skin that prevents them from drying out.

PAINTED TURTLE

WOOD TURTLE

NORTHERN WATER SNAKE

SPLOOSH

GURGLE

SPLASH!

AT NIGHTFALL, the young beaver leaves the shelter of the shoreline to begin work on the old dam. She concentrates on one area where she hears water spilling gently over the top of the pile.

First she gathers some branches to plug the large gaps.

Then she swims down to the bottom of the stream, where she scoops up muck and leaves to pack between the layers of branches.

She stacks the new material higher and higher. She listens again for any other place where water is still leaking through the dam.

She works through the night.

As dawn appears, she takes a break to find a place to rest for the day.

CHICK-A-DEE-DEE-DEE!

She tucks herself beneath an overhanging bank, safely hidden behind a shallow island of sedges and other delicious plants. Tonight she will continue making this place into a home of her own.

HANDY NEIGHBORS

The habitat around beaver ponds is well suited for raccoons. Like beavers, raccoons are most active at night.

Raccoons have sharp FRONT TEETH for biting and flatter teeth in back for chewing.

They are **omnivores**, which means they eat a wide range of plants and animals.

The BLACK MASK and RINGED TAIL may serve as camouflage.

Raccoons have very sensitive FRONT FEET that help them learn about their environment at night. They use their hands to swim, grab food, dig, climb, and even open containers.

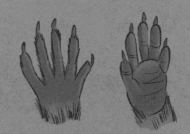

LATER IN THE AFTERNOON, the young beaver begins another full night of dam building. Already the water level behind the dam has risen, creating a small pond. That makes it easier to swim to the birches and willows along the stream edge.

She is chewing down a small willow when a loud *SLAP!* shifts her attention down the stream. It sounds like another beaver!

Instinctively she plunges into the water, heading the other way.

SLAP!

SPLOOSH!

SNIFF SNIFF SNIFF

When she surfaces upstream, she lets only the very top of her head, eyes, ears, and nose show. With her poor eyesight, she cannot see very far. She pauses and sniffs. Could there be another beaver in this place?

She listens for danger. Hearing none, she swims cautiously back toward the dam. It smells like a male beaver is nearby, so she moves slowly toward his scent.

Suddenly, there he is, only a few feet away.

PURRR

WHINE

The other beaver does not want to compete either. He is also two years old and has just left his family, looking for a new place to live.

They make soft whining noises back and forth. She takes in his unique smell.

SNIFF

SNIFF

In the days that follow, they work together to establish this pond as their territory. Together they can build up the dam more quickly.

EVEN THOUGH IT'S SUMMER, the beavers must prepare for the next winter. A sheltered area of the bank, where the water is deep, is a good place to start building a lodge.

SQUISH SCRATCH

The young beaver swims underwater and scoops out the soft mud of the shore with her front feet. It easily gives way.

She tunnels into the bank, avoiding the large, strong roots of a white pine stump.

For hours each night, the two beavers take turns digging until the underwater entrance is several feet long.

Then they burrow upward to construct a small platform, raised up out of the water.

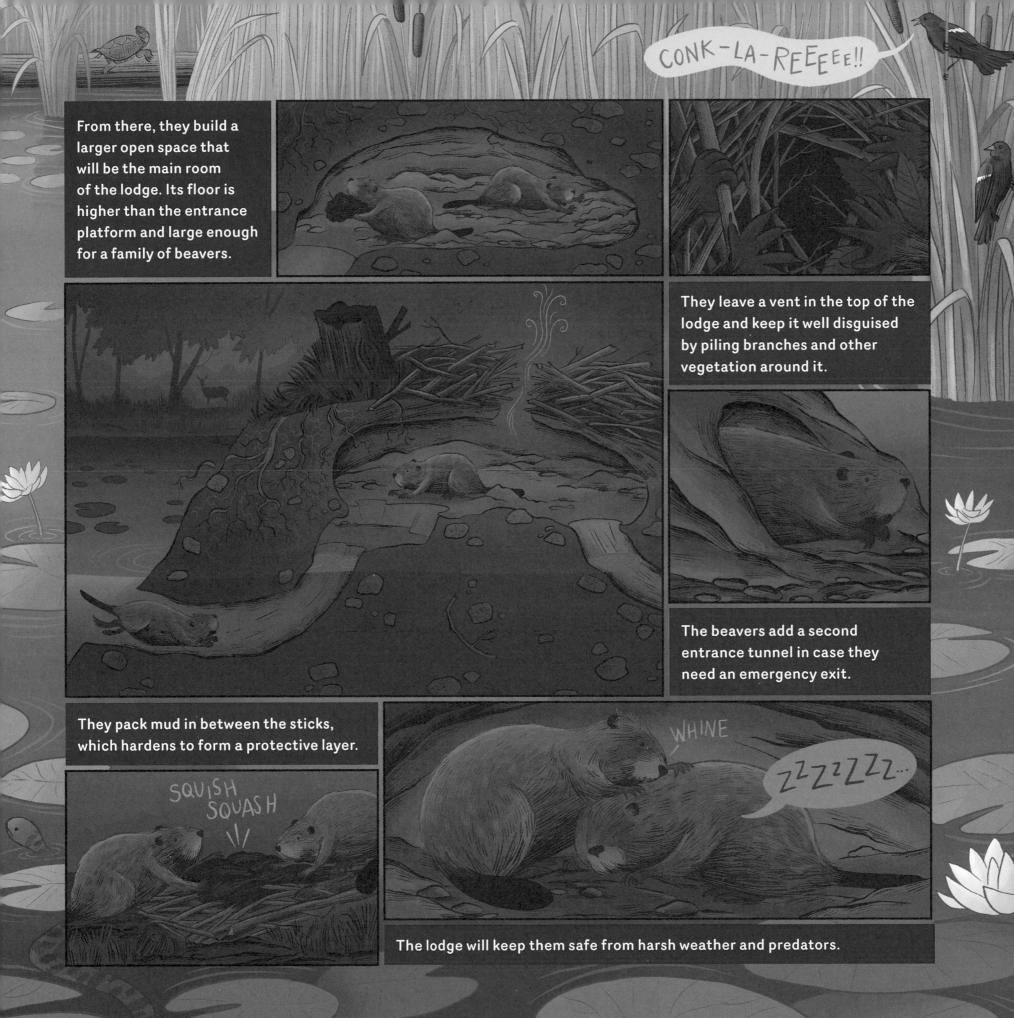

CONK-LA-REEEEE!!

From there, they build a larger open space that will be the main room of the lodge. Its floor is higher than the entrance platform and large enough for a family of beavers.

They leave a vent in the top of the lodge and keep it well disguised by piling branches and other vegetation around it.

The beavers add a second entrance tunnel in case they need an emergency exit.

They pack mud in between the sticks, which hardens to form a protective layer.

SQUISH SQUASH

WHINE

ZZZZZZZ...

The lodge will keep them safe from harsh weather and predators.

IN THE EVENINGS, both beavers build scent mounds along the boundary of their new territory. These mounds alert other beavers that a family already lives here.

dam

scent mounds

food cache

bank lodge

Building a scent mound is a lot of work.

With his front feet, the young male beaver collects leaves, sticks, and mud from the bottom of the pond.

He carries the material onto the shore and pushes it into a pile. He adds dry leaves to make the pile higher.

PFFFTT

SNIFF SNIFF

He marks the pile with his special scent, called castoreum. With a loud gassy sound, he squirts a slimy yellow-brown liquid from the castor glands at the base of his tail. Castoreum smells good, sort of like vanilla. The female beaver also marks the mounds.

ALL SUMMER LONG, the two beavers feast on the plants in the pond and along its edges. They can smell which are the best to eat. Every day, they crunch on cattails and sedges.

From the mucky bottom, they pull up thick, rope-like stems of water lily and search for one of their favorite foods, duck potato.

They carry the plants out of the water and spread them across a log to eat them.

The beavers chew down the small trees and shrubs at the water's edge. Their favorites are aspen, willow, and birch. They eat the leaves, twigs, and inner bark.

As summer turns to fall, they begin storing food for the winter in a giant food cache outside the lodge. They harvest thousands of branches to last several months.

To reach more trees, they raise the water level by building the dam higher. They dig side channels so they can swim to new areas with young trees.

Every evening they cut down more trees, including large ones.

WHAT'S FOR BREAKFAST?

Beavers' favorite foods change with the seasons. They'll eat leaves, flowers, roots, and, especially, inner bark. They look for food in or near the water, so they won't have to walk too far on land. They use some trees for food. They use other trees for building materials.

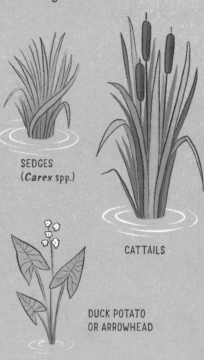

SEDGES
(*Carex* spp.)

CATTAILS

DUCK POTATO OR ARROWHEAD

WATER LILIES

ASPEN

BIRCH

WILLOW

ONE RAINY NIGHT, the two beavers work together to take down a large yellow birch tree. The trunk is so wide that they each work on their own side, chewing quickly.

Turning her head, the young beaver bites into the wood with the side of her mouth. She bites again and again.

Rain begins to fall as the beavers work. Now there are deep, angled cuts all the way around the trunk, but the tree does not fall over.

A blast of wind pushes so hard against the treetop that the whole birch bends toward the water.

The beavers listen. They must be careful that the tree does not fall on them.

The wind picks up. A huge gust slams the birch and it begins to topple.

POP!

CRACK!

SPLASH!

The beavers dive into the water just in time to avoid the tree as it crashes down heavily. They will come back when the storm passes to continue their work.

TOUGH TEETH!

Beaver teeth never stop growing. They use their front teeth to eat the inner bark of a branch, like nibbling corn on the cob.

To chew down large trees, beavers use their front teeth at an angle.

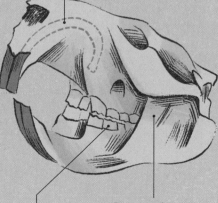

The front surface of a beaver tooth is harder than the back. The uneven wear of the teeth keeps the edges sharp.

The sharp INCISORS grow from deep inside the skull.

Beavers have very strong jaw muscles.

MOLARS are good for grinding wood.

AS THE SEASON CHANGES, the two beavers work day and night to complete all of their important tasks before winter.

The young beaver drags a large poplar branch into the water. Diving deep, she wedges it into the base of the winter food cache. The top part will freeze into the ice, so they put the tastiest food at the bottom.

The pair adds more mud and sticks to make the lodge cozy, secure, and well camouflaged. The outside must be as strong as cement.

CHICK-A-
DEE-DEE-
DEE!

CACHING FOOD

The beavers aren't the only animals who gather food to last through the long months of winter. Chipmunks store piles of acorns and other seeds in their underground tunnels. Red squirrels sometimes dry mushrooms before hiding them.

RED SQUIRREL

CHIPMUNK

WHITE-FOOTED
MOUSE

GRAY
SQUIRREL

The dam must keep the water level high enough so the beavers can live safely below the frozen surface all winter long.

JEER! JEER! JEER!

RAT-A-TAT-TAT!

A red-bellied woodpecker hides food in a tree.

A family of blue jays helps their young fledglings learn to find food.

CONK-LA-REE!

CHUCK! CHUCK!

Gray squirrels bury nuts to feast on during the winter.

Blue jays hide seeds in the ground. Woodpeckers, nuthatches, and titmice store seeds in holes or cracks in tree bark.

RED-BELLIED WOODPECKER

PILEATED WOODPECKER

BLUE JAY

WHITE-BREASTED NUTHATCH

TUFTED TITMOUSE

ONE EVENING IN NOVEMBER, as the sun sets and snow flurries come down, the two beavers rest inside the lodge.

CRUNCH!

CRUNCH!

ZZZZZzz...

SNOOOOOZE

Suddenly they hear something LOUD right outside. They stay very still, listening and sniffing for clues.

They hear snorting and digging—is something trying to get inside?

SNORT! SNORT!

The lodge shakes. A large animal is pounding on it. The beavers get ready to escape through their underwater exit.

After a few terrifying seconds, the pummeling stops. Has the predator given up? The beavers stay inside the lodge for several minutes, listening.

Once it is quiet, they venture outside. All around the lodge are the large, deep tracks of a black bear.

In a few places, the bear's claws have ripped branches off the lodge. Luckily, it is well built, and the beavers are safe.

WHAT DO BLACK BEARS EAT?

Bears eat many different foods. Their excellent sense of smell helps them find berries, nuts, and other plants. They will eat dead animals and sometimes hunt, as this bear is doing.

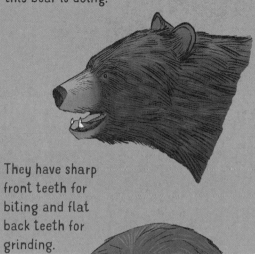

They have sharp front teeth for biting and flat back teeth for grinding.

With their huge claws, they tear apart rotting logs and dig in the ground, looking for grubs and insects.

THE REST OF WINTER is a quiet time for the pair. The animal world around the pond feels still. Many animals are sheltered in dens or tree cavities, only coming out for short periods of time.

The bear snoozes in its den. Raccoons stay cozy in hollow trees or burrows.

Deer seek shelter in hemlock groves where the snow isn't as deep. The red fox keeps warm with a thick coat and fluffy tail.

Chickadees, titmice, and other birds flock together for protection. They fluff up their feathers for warmth.

The beavers spend their time grooming and resting inside the lodge. When they're hungry, they swim below the ice to retrieve food from the cache.

WHO COOKS FOR YOU?

In the spring, the young beavers will begin the cycle again. They may even start a family of their own.

DEAR READER,

I am very curious about beavers, and I bet you are, too. Curiosity is at the heart of this book. Over the years, I have spent thousands of hours watching and learning about beavers and their habitat.

What do they like to eat?

Where do they build their homes?

How do they cross a road?

Who else lives in a beaver pond?

I've learned a lot, but there is so much more to discover!

If there is a pond you can investigate, start exploring. Ask yourself plenty of questions:

Are there clues that a beaver lives here or has lived here? What are they?

How is the pond different during winter and fall?

What kinds of plants grow near the water?

Many other animals live in and around a beaver pond, and some of them are included in this book. You may not see them all, but if you look and listen closely, you will get to know their signs.

Be prepared to keep exploring, because just when you think you have figured it all out, you might find something that makes you ask, "What Goes On inside a Beaver Pond?"

Wishing you joyful and curious adventures,

Becky

The mission of Storey Publishing is to serve our customers by publishing practical information that encourages personal independence in harmony with the environment.

Edited by Hannah Fries, Lisa H. Hiley, and Deborah Burns

Art direction and book design by Jessica Armstrong

Text production by Jennifer Jepson Smith

Illustrations by © Carrie Shryock

The editors would like to thank Donovan Smith, whose curiosity and love of nature inspired this book.

Text © 2023 by Becky Cushing Gop

Storey books are available at special discounts when purchased in bulk for premiums and sales promotions as well as for fund-raising or educational use. Special editions or book excerpts can also be created to specification. For details, please send an email to special.markets@hbgusa.com.

Storey Publishing
210 MASS MoCA Way
North Adams, MA 01247
storey.com

Storey Publishing, LLC is an imprint of Workman Publishing Co., Inc., a subsidiary of Hachette Book Group, Inc., 1290 Avenue of the Americas, New York, NY 10104

Distributed in Europe by Hachette Livre, 58 rue Jean Bleuzen, 92 178 Vanves Cedex, France

Distributed in the United Kingdom by Hachette Book Group, UK, Carmelite House, 50 Victoria Embankment, London EC4Y 0DZ

ISBNs: 978-1-63586-527-1 (hardcover); 978-1-63586-528-8 (ebook); 978-1-63586-794-7 (ebook); 978-1-63586-795-4 (ebook)

Printed in China through Asia Pacific Offset

10 9 8 7 6 5 4 3 2 1

Library of Congress Cataloging-in-Publication Data on file

Can you find these animals in this book?

AMERICAN TOAD

CADDISFLY

GRAY TREE FROG

RACCOON

TUFTED TITMOUSE

BARRED OWL

CANADA GOOSE

JEFFERSON SALAMANDER

RED-BELLIED WOODPECKER

WATER STRIDER

BELTED KINGFISHER

CARDINAL

LITTLE BROWN BAT

RED FOX

WHIRLIGIG BEETLE

BLACK BEAR

CHIPMUNK

LUNA MOTH

RED SQUIRREL

WHITE-BREASTED NUTHATCH

BLACK-CAPPED CHICKADEE

COMMON YELLOWTHROAT

MINK

RED-TAILED HAWK

WHITE-FOOTED MOUSE

GREAT BLUE HERON

COYOTE

MOSQUITO

RED-WINGED BLACKBIRD

WHITE-TAILED DEER

BLUE JAY

DRAGONFLY

NORTHERN WATER SNAKE

SNAPPING TURTLE

WOOD DUCK

BOBCAT

GREEN FROG

PAINTED TURTLE

SPOTTED SALAMANDER

WOOD FROG

BULLFROG

HERMIT THRUSH

PICKEREL FROG

SPRING PEEPER

WOOD TURTLE

BULLHEAD

GRAY SQUIRREL

PILEATED WOODPECKER

STONEFLY

YELLOW WARBLER